Go to Bed, Ted!

by Marie Powell

illustrated by Amy Cartwright

amicus readers

1

Say Hello to Amicus Readers.

You'll find our helpful dog, Amicus, chasing a ball—to let you know the reading level of a book.

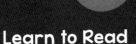

1 Learn to Read

Frequent repetition, high frequency words, and close photo-text matches introduce familiar topics and provide ample support for brand new readers.

2 Read Independently

Some repetition is mixed with varied sentence structures and a select amount of new vocabulary words are introduced with text and photo support.

3 Read to Know More

Interesting facts and engaging art and photos give fluent readers fun books both for reading practice and to learn about new topics.

Amicus Readers are published by Amicus
P.O. Box 1329, Mankato, MN 56002
www.amicuspublishing.us

Illustrations by Amy Cartwright

Produced for Amicus by The Peterson Publishing Company and Red Line Editorial.

Editor Jenna Gleisner
Designer Craig Hinton
Printed in the United States of America
North Mankato, MN
10 9 8 7 6 5 4 3 2 1

Library of Congress Cataloging-in-Publication Data
Powell, Marie, 1958-
  Go to bed, Ted! / by Marie Powell ; illustrated by Amy Cartwright.
    pages cm. -- (Word Families)
  Summary: "Young readers meet Ted, a boy who refuses to go to bed, while learning words in the -ed word family."
  Audience: K to Grade 3.
  ISBN 978-1-60753-927-8 (hardcover) --
  ISBN 978-1-68151-051-4 (pdf ebook)
  1. English language--Phonetics--Juvenile literature. 2. Vocabulary--Juvenile literature. 3. Reading--Phonetic method. 4. Readers (Primary) I. Cartwright, Amy, illustrator. II. Title.
  PE1135.P6385 2016
  428'.1--dc23
                                                    2015033472

"It is getting late. Time for bed, Ted," Mom said.

"You too, Ed."

"Just one more ride on the sled!" said Ted. "Put your sled in the shed, Ted," Mom said. "It is time for bed."

5

Ted put on his pajamas.
But he would not go
to **bed**.
"First I want my stuffed
bear, **Fred**," said **Ted**.
Ted sped down to the
kitchen to find **Fred**.

"Can I have a snack?"
pled Ted.

"Okay. But then it is time for **bed**, **Ted**," said Mom. But **Ted** still would not go to **bed**.

"Can I have a story, please?" pled Ted. Ted handed Mom his favorite book.

But after she read, Ted
still would not go to **bed**.

"Can you help, Ed?" asked Mom.
Ed knew what Ted wanted. Ed hunted in the closet for the **red** night-light.

Ed plugged in the **red** light.
"Now go to **bed**, Ted,"
Ed said. But Ted had
already **drifted** off
to sleep.

Word Family: -ed

Word families are groups of words that rhyme and are spelled the same.

Here are the -ed words in this book:

bed	red
drifted	shed
Ed	sled
Fred	sped
handed	Ted
hunted	wanted
pled	

Can you spell any other words with -ed?